W9-ANN-926

Utah
The Beehive State

Marcia Amidon
Lusted

PowerKiDS press™

New York

For Steve, Kathy, and Kitsel

Published in 2011 by The Rosen Publishing Group, Inc.
29 East 21st Street, New York, NY 10010

First Edition

Editor: Maggie Murphy
Book Design: Greg Tucker
Photo Researcher: Jessica Gerweck

Photo Credits: Cover, pp. 5, 9, 11, 15, 17, 19, 22 (animal, flag) Shutterstock.com; p. 7 M.L. Harris/ Getty Images; p. 13 Johannes Kroemer/Getty Images; p. 22 (tree) www.iStockphoto.com/Stephanie Howard; p. 22 (bird) www.iStockphoto.com/Nickolay Stanev; p. 22 (flower) Wikimedia Commons; p. 22 (Marie Osmond) Ethan Miller/Getty Images; p. 22 (Philo Farnsworth) Time & Life Pictures/Getty Images; p. 22 (Jewel Kilcher) Charley Gallay/Getty Images.

Library of Congress Cataloging-in-Publication Data

Lusted, Marcia Amidon.
  Utah : the beehive state / Marcia Amidon Lusted. — 1st ed.
      p. cm. — (Our amazing states)
  Includes index.
  ISBN 978-1-4488-0660-7 (library binding) — ISBN 978-1-4488-0752-9 (pbk.) — ISBN 978-1-4488-0753-6 (6-pack)
  1. Utah—Juvenile literature. I. Title.
  F826.3.L87 2011
  979.2—dc22
                                    2009048698

Manufactured in the United States of America

CPSIA Compliance Information: Batch #WS10PK: For Further Information contact Rosen Publishing, New York, New York at 1-800-237-9932

Contents

Land of the Honeybee

There is a place where you can find deserts, mountains, and a great lake filled with salt. You can find dinosaur **fossils** and wagon tracks from **pioneers**. The 2002 Olympic Winter Games were held there. Where are you? You are in Utah!

Utah is located in the western part of the United States. It is surrounded by six other states, with Colorado to the east and Nevada to the west. The Colorado River runs across the southeast corner of the state.

Utah got its nickname, the Beehive State, from the early **Mormon** settlers. They wanted to call the state Deseret, a term used in a Mormon holy book to mean "honeybee." The name Utah comes from the name of the Native American Ute people.

Here you can see a part of Zion National Park, one of the five national parks in Utah. The United States Congress made Zion a national park in 1919.

Going West

The first people to live in Utah were Native Americans such as the Anasazis. They built their homes high in the walls of **canyons**. Later peoples included the Utes, the Paiutes, the Shoshones, the Goshutes, and the Navajos. Mexican and Spanish **explorers** were the first outsiders to visit Utah.

A **religious** group known as the Mormons came to Utah in 1847. They settled in the Salt Lake Valley and built their first town, Salt Lake City. Each family was given land to build a house and start a farm.

Many other pioneers also settled in Utah and the area grew. In 1868, at Promontory Point, the Central Pacific and Union Pacific railroad tracks met. For the first time, there was a railroad line all the way across the country.

These are the ruins of an ancient Anasazi home in Bullet Canyon, Utah. The home, called a kiva, was built into the rocky cliff seen here.

Snow and Salt Flats

Utah has many different types of land. The snowy tops of the Rocky Mountains curve through the state. The Colorado River flows through the hot, dry Canyonlands with its flat **mesas** and canyons.

An ancient lake called Lake Bonneville once covered most of Utah. While most of the lake dried up about 14,500 years ago, the Great Salt Lake is the largest part of what remains of it. In western Utah, the ancient lake left behind hard salt crystals, now called the Bonneville Salt Flats.

Utah is sunny and warm for most of the year, although winters can be cold and snowy. The Rocky Mountain area gets as much as 60 inches (150 cm) of rain and snow every year. However, dry areas might get only 5 inches (13 cm) of rain.

The Bonneville Salt Flats, shown here, cover more than 30,000 acres (12,141 ha) of land in northwestern Utah.

Lizards, Cougars, and Seagulls, Oh My!

Many different kinds of plants grow in Utah. The dry areas have prickly pear cactus, saltbush, and creosote. Blue spruce and quaking aspen grow in the mountains.

In Utah's deserts, lizards and rattlesnakes can be found, as well as kangaroo rats, which hop on their back legs like kangaroos. In the mountains, cougars, bobcats, mule deer, and foxes roam. Carp, catfish, and trout swim in Utah's rivers and lakes.

Barn owls, hawks, and magpies fly through Utah's skies. The state bird is the California seagull. This bird eats brine shrimp from the Great Salt Lake. A group of these birds once saved the early settlers' crops by eating a **swarm** of insects that came into the Salt Lake Valley.

The Rocky Mountain elk is Utah's state animal. This is a bull, or male, elk. A bull elk's antlers can weigh up to 40 pounds (18 kg).

Made in Utah

Farming is one of Utah's biggest **industries**. Farmers raise beef cattle and produce milk from dairy cows. Wool and honey are also important. Crops like hay, wheat, barley, and fruit are grown, as well as mushrooms and safflowers.

Mining is another big industry. Steel, aluminum, and copper are mined there, as well as coal, uranium, and petroleum. Utah's factories make computers and electronics. Government **agencies**, as well as the Army and the Air Force, provide jobs for many people in Utah.

Tourism is growing in the state. Many people visit Utah every year to ski. Tourists also visit Park City for the Sundance Film Festival, which is held there every year.

These children are riding a ski lift to the top of a ski slope in Brighton, Utah. Many skiiers and snowboarders in Utah are visitors to the state.

The Crossroads of the West

Utah's capital is Salt Lake City, the city founded by the Mormons in 1847. Some people call it the Crossroads of the West. The Mormon temple, which took 40 years to build, is located in Temple Square. The temple and the state capitol were built with rock from Utah.

There are many things to do in Salt Lake City. You can visit the Pioneer Memorial Museum or the Old Deseret Historical Village. The Children's Museum of Utah has hands-on displays.

Near Salt Lake City are Promontory Point and the Golden Spike National Historic Site. This is the place where the golden final spike of the **transcontinental** railroad was hammered into place. Two **replica** steam engines are on display there.

The Salt Lake Temple, shown here, was completed in 1893, three years before Utah became a state.

Salty Waters

Utah's Great Salt Lake is the largest saltwater lake in North America. It is a small part of the ancient Lake Bonneville, which existed during the Ice Age. Because no water streams flow out of the lake, its water is very salty. Fresh water coming in **evaporates**, leaving the salt behind.

The Great Salt Lake is too salty for fish to live in. Only some algae and brine shrimp can live in its waters. However, because it has many wetlands, many different types of birds nest there.

The lake also has a work of art called the *Spiral Jetty*. Made of black rock piled in a curled shape, it reaches out in the water. It was created by artist Robert Smithson in 1970.

This is Antelope Island, in the Great Salt Lake. Antelope Island is a Utah state park. Wild bison, pronghorn sheep, and bighorn sheep roam freely on this island.

Under the Arches

One of Utah's most amazing places is **Arches** National Park, in southeast Utah. Here there are more than 2,000 natural sandstone arches. They were created when wind and water wore away the sandstone and made different shapes. The arches and cliffs have many beautiful colors and textures.

Ancient peoples once roamed the Arches area to collect rocks to make tools. In 1929, the government began protecting the area. Today, almost a million people visit the park every year.

Visitors can hike through the Fiery Furnace. It has with narrow passages and dead ends among sandstone cliffs and fins. Fins are a kind of sandstone landform. Rangers guide tourists to help protect plants and landforms.

There are several famous sandstone arches at Arches National Park. This one is called the North Window.

Come to Utah!

Whether you want to boat on Lake Powell, which was created when the Glen Canyon Dam was built, or search for dinosaur fossils at the Dinosaur National Monument, Utah has something for you. If you visit the Four Corners, you can even touch parts of four states at once! Here the corners of Arizona, New Mexico, Utah, and Colorado meet.

You can ski Utah's mountains or climb its arches and hoodoos, which are rock shapes formed by wind and rain. You might also like to view the night sky through a telescope at the Hansen Planetarium in Salt Lake City. With its beautiful scenery and great things to do, Utah is a wonderful place to visit or live!

Glossary

agencies (AY-jen-seez) Special departments of the government.

arches (AHRCH-ez) Shapes that curve at the top and make openings.

canyons (KAN-yunz) Deep, narrow valleys.

evaporates (ih-VA-puh-rayts) Changes from a liquid to a gas.

explorers (ek-SPLOR-erz) People who travel and look for new land.

fossils (FO-sulz) The hardened remains of dead animals or plants.

industries (IN-dus-treez) Businesses in which many people work and make money producing a product.

mesas (MAY-suz) Hills or mountains with flat tops.

Mormon (MOR-mun) Belonging to a church that was founded in the United States by Joseph Smith in 1830.

pioneers (py-uh-NEERZ) Some of the first people to settle in a new area.

religious (rih-LIH-jus) Faithful to a religion and its beliefs.

replica (REH-plih-kuh) An exact copy of an object used in the past, such as an artifact or a building.

swarm (SWORM) A large number of insects, often in motion.

tourism (TUR-ih-zem) A business that deals with people who travel for pleasure.

transcontinental (trants-kon-tuh-NEN-tul) Going across a continent.

Utah State Symbols

State Tree
Blue Spruce

State Animal
Rocky Mountain
Elk

State Flag

State Bird
California Seagull

State Flower
Sego Lily

State Seal

Famous People from Utah

Philo T. Farnsworth
(1906–1971)
Born in Beaver, UT
Inventor of the Television

Marie Osmond
(1959–)
Born in Ogden, UT
Singer/Actress

Jewel Kilcher
(1974–)
Born in Payson, UT
Singer-Songwriter

Utah State Map

Legend

○ Major City

✪ Capital

〰 River

Logan

Great Salt Lake

Ogden

Salt Lake City

Wasatch Range

Uinta Mountains

Utah Lake

Provo

Vernal

Green River

Price

Roan Cliffs

Wah Wah Mountains

Sevier Lake

Moab

Henry Mountains

Colorado River

Lake Powell

San Juan River

Utah State Facts

Population: About 2,233,169

Area: 84,916 square miles (219,931 sq km)

Motto: "Industry"

Song: "Utah, This Is the Place," words by Sam and Gary Francis and music by Gary Francis

Index

Web Sites

Due to the changing nature of Internet links, PowerKids Press has developed an online list of Web sites related to the subject of this book. This site is updated regularly. Please use this link to access the list:

www.powerkidslinks.com/amst/ut/